CW00864210

Forsake *All* ^{to} Gain *All*

The Benefits of Living a Holy Lifestyle

LINDA ROSS

BALBOA
PRESS
A DIVISION OF HAY HOUSE

Balboa Press books may be ordered through booksellers or by contacting:

Balboa Press
A Division of Hay House
1663 Liberty Drive
Bloomington, IN 47403
www.balboapress.com
1 (877) 407-4847

Print information available on the last page.

ISBN: 978-1-9822-2409-7 (sc)
ISBN: 978-1-9822-2411-0 (hc)
ISBN: 978-1-9822-2410-3 (e)

Library of Congress Control Number: 2019903448

Balboa Press rev. date: 04/26/2019

Contents

Bandage

We have all been in relationships that have left scars on the inside of our heart, soul and body, that shampoo, soap, makeup or even a facelift can't cover up or wash away.

We camouflage ourselves with beautiful clothes, cars, jobs, homes, even fake smiles, trying to exist each day without the ability to know how to really live, we just go through the emotions and keep moving.

The scars we possess are open wounds never healing, just getting covered daily by the bandages of life that we hide so well.

These scars of life form us into who we are.

Many times, we cry inside not able to forget the hurt of our past, buried deep inside our soul. It could be that old song or that place our mind takes us into, we may even see a child across the room reminding us of ourselves, we then began to rehearse the pain all over again, their eyes reminding us of what happened so long ago.

When we practice our hurt, we expose ourselves to punishment, often reliving the hurt and pain over again like pouring alcohol on an open wound, robbing ourselves from becoming the real person we are destined to be, we not only keep ourselves in bondage, we deprive others as well, it's a vicious cycle.

This person that was so well covered with bandages was me, the scars of life had me down for a while, I could not see any truth or think clearly, my whole life was a cover up with bandages.

One day God set me free, and I want to share with you how to get totally free without the use of any more band-aids, only a pill, the (Gos pill) Gospel.

Bandages cover open wounds, protecting the sore from all unclean elements, even though we put bandages on for protection we must take them off to finish the healing process, after a while we began to see a scab form and before long it starts to itch, and later the scab is gone, and only a scar remains of what use to be.

When we cover our wounds in life, we only camouflage our hurts, hiding them, and we become accustom to wearing a mask.

When reliving the hurt in our mind, we are nurturing a thought, we continue to punish ourselves in pain, by rehearsing and rethinking what we need so desperately to forget.

To begin the healing process, we must forgive the person that wronged or betrayed us. We must renew our mind.

So, let the healing begin!

How to Forgive

One day while reading the word of God I read in Ephesians chapter one verse seven "In whom we have redemption through his blood, the forgiveness of sins according to the riches of his grace." Praise God for his grace, also in First John chapter one verse nine it says, "If we confess our sins, he is faithful and just to forgive us our sins and to cleanse us from all unrighteousness." Now that's good news, all we have to do is confess our sin and turn away from them. Remember God so loved the world that he gave his only begotten son and who ever believes on him should not perish but have everlasting life.

Jesus gave his life, so that we could have eternal life.

The Lord forgave us, we can forgive others, because as he is so are, we in this world.

To forgive is to pardon that person of all wrongs, to have no ill feelings against them or the situation that has occurred.

When you forget you don't rehearse the thing in your mind, each time the hurt of what has happen surfaces in your mind you need to cast it down, not entertaining the thought, that means you don't occupy the thought in your mind or let it absorb or hold your attention.

When you entertain a thought, you bring it back to life, reliving it over in your mind, you bring it back into existence, this is when all the hurt resurfaces.

To forgive is to have no resentment towards that person, to overlook what they have done, pardoning them and releasing them from any punishment or wrongs they committed against you, this will free that person from whatever they have done.

This sounds so good, but to actually to do this is another thing!

Some may say I don't feel any forgiveness in my heart, remember we do not live by feelings or emotions we live by what the word of God says for our life, and prayer does changes things.

Just to give you a testimony on forgiving, I'll tell you my very own story.

As a teenager I was raped by a man I trusted somewhat, this act of violation shaped my way of thinking in many areas of my life. As I got older I pushed this in the back on my mind, I thought I had forgiven this man, only to realize when I went to the movies (twenty five years later) with a couple of girlfriends, all the feelings I had about getting raped, began to resurface, just this one movie bought back feelings of bitterness, hurt shame and betrayal, tears began to flow down my face, of course my friends wanted to know what in the world was wrong with me, I had to tell them, just like the little girl in the movie got raped, so did I.

As I began to talk more about what had happen in my life to them and others, it began to release the hurt, and the word of God healed me, and gave me a heart to forgive this man, from all wrongs he had done. I started looking at this man in a different perspective, maybe he was lustful, hurt or raped when he was a child, or even a whoremonger, all I knew was in order for me to go on in life and to release this shame, bitterness and hurt out of my heart, I had to move on forgiving, and releasing him for all the wrong doing he had done to me, you see not only was I holding him in bondage, but I was holding myself as well.

An unforgiving heart causes bitterness, resentment and pain, even sickness in your body. I had to remember, if Jesus forgive the beating and pain he went through, I knew I had to forgive this man and anyone else, for any wrongs they did to me, or to the people I loved.

When we don't forgive, we never release that person to be free, we continually cleave to what they have done to us, we hold them captive.

Pray and ask the Lord to come into your heart, to heal the hurt so you can forgive and release that person.

Speak what you want to manifest

Start speaking forgiveness, saying aloud, I forgive this person for all the wrongs they have committed in my life, or the life of my love ones, Lord I thank you, for forgiving me for all the wrongs I have done to others, I release this person in the name of Jesus, and I am moving on to my divine destiny God has planned for my life, in Jesus name amen.

A lot of times when we forgive people, we still have a fear of the reoccurrence from that person, a fear of not making it on our own without their presence in our life, we may not even realize we are living in fear, because it has become a part of our everyday life.

To live in fear, is having a spirit of fear, let us take a look and see if we are living in fear or trusting God for our life.

2 Timothy 1:17 says; "For God hath not given us the spirit of fear; but of power, and of love, and of a sound mind."

Fear paralyzes, it will stop you right in your tracks, it will rob you of your ability to move forward, or make the right decisions, it deprives you from ever reaching your destiny, I know because I lived in fear for years.

The word fear means, to be afraid, full of fright, to be terrified.

Fear keeps you in panic mode, worrying and becoming anxious over what is happening in the now, and what is going to take place in your future, fear is trusting in your own ability, trusting in the things you can see, hear, smell, feel or touch.

When you live in fear you sometimes, build your life on your emotions and not on what the true word of God says for your life.

Fear is based on unbelief.

Trusting the Lord for your life eliminates fear, trusting him keeps you stable and unwavering, secure in his ability and not your own, trusting God keeps you in a restful state, knowing that whatever he has said, he is able to perform.

We must Love one another

When you love someone, you feel affection towards them, most of the time having a desire to provide, protect, support and nurture them, we try to improve their lives because of the love we have towards them. When we love people, you want the best for them, our love is sincere.

I want to make a point about love, as Christians, we sometimes think we are only to love people that are living for the Lord, we tell ourselves if they are not like me, then I want nothing to do with them, I have never heard people actually say these things, but there actions speak for themselves, if you think back, and I'm sure some of you, could give a testimony about how you smoked, stole, drank or even cursed people out.

Oh yeah now I remember!

Jesus came not to condemn the world, but to save the world.

The Word of God says, as he is, so are we in this world.

He loved the unlovable, the sick, lame, blind, and the ones that had demons in them, people need to see the love of Christ in us.

At one time or another we were just like them, we lived sinful lives, we didn't desire to have God in our life, we were doing our own thing.

Remember, we are constantly getting delivered in areas of our lives.

We must love the hurt out of each other.

Love is a commandment not a choice.

This is my commandment, that ye love one another, as I have loved you."

More scriptures to read are Romans 13:8 and 1John 4:8.

The Only Pill That Heals

I have tried so many things in my life to attain peace and contentment, even the love from others, I felt so misunderstood, I could've saved myself so much precious time, just by letting the word of God do the work instead of trusting in my own ability. My personal bandages covered all my flaws, to look perfect and complete, putting on a fakeness that only covered all the shame, hurt and pain that no one knew I lived.

When I found out how much my father God loved me, I broke down and cried like a baby and I still do. He began to show me how complete I am in him, and he has a divine destiny for me, I have a desire to tell people about the word of God, about our savior Jesus.

I know out of my belly flows rivers of living water into the lives of others, you see God sent me here to be a blessing to so many people, I impact the lives of others and so do you, he has a plan for your life, so take off the bandages, all the coverings, and let the healing began.

Let go and let God, it is in his ability, not ours, trust him to do what you cannot do, he will never leave you, nor will he ever forsake you.

Remember you are not your own, you were bought for a price, you didn't come cheap, he paid a big price, he gave his life in exchange for our life. He said I came to give you life, and to give it more abundantly, so rejoice, in who he is and what he has planned for your life. As the old song writer says; It is no secret what God can do, what he's done for others he will do for you.

Read the word of God, faith comes by hearing and hearing by the word of God, we must have a relationship with him, trust in his leading, let the holy spirit lead you, pray and forgive others, get counsel from godly people, renew your mind and love.

Remember you can do all things through Christ who strengthens you.

Keeping Our Body for Jesus

We all need each other in the body of Christ.

We are one body functioning together.

I am going to attempt to talk to you about the human body, in comparison to the spiritual body. In addition, I would like to mention that I know very little about the function of the human body.

The human body has many functions, the hand can't smell, the eyes cannot hear, and the feet cannot taste, we all know that the nose is for smelling, and the eyes are what we see with, and the ears are for hearing.

Every part of our body has a different function, these different functions, work together to keep our body operating in the correct way. Our bodies cannot function correctly without organs, blood, body fluids, tissues and other things.

Everything inside our body is for a purpose, coming together to function at its fullest capability. Sometimes when the body is not functioning at its fullest capability, it affects other organs in our body to not function correctly.

In the body of Christ there is many members, we are all in the same body, but we all have different functions not the same office, read Romans chapter twelve verse four.

In first Corinthians chapter twelve verses 1-27 it explains about spiritual gifts in the body of Christ. The spiritual body has many members, the natural body has many organs.

In the body of Christ there is given many gifts to members, to one is given by the spirit a gift of healing, another the gift of wisdom, prophecy or the working of miracles, divers kinds of tongues and the interpretation of tongues, but as the scripture says in first Corinthians chapter twelve, verse eleven, "But all these work that one and the selfsame Spirit, dividing to every man severally as he will."

God places us in the body where we are needed; we all have gifts that are given by God for edifying and building up and serving in the body, we are all members of the same body with different gifts, to make the body function in fulness.

In the body of Christ, we all need each other; if one suffers, we all suffer.

All are important in the body of Christ, no one should think of themselves as more important than others.

Let us look at the word edify.

Edify means to build, care, to instruct, as to improve or uplift.

We are to build up one another and be concerned about one another, loving and uplifting each other, we are to help our brothers and sisters, to attain a higher spiritual level in Christ, when building each other up, we are inspiring, motivating and encouraging each other.

Now it says in I Corinthians chapter fourteen verse twelve, "Even so ye, forasmuch as ye are zealous of spiritual gifts, seek that ye may excel to the edifying of the church."

It is a good thing to have spiritual gifts, but what good is it doing, if we do not have love in our hearts, one for another.

You cannot minister about something that you are not living.

Now let us get back to our topic, keeping our body for Jesus.

God said let our body be a living sacrifice, holy and acceptable to him, we are the very temple of the living God, we are not our own, we were bought for a price, Jesus paid that price when he died on calvary, and took sin, death, sickness and diseases in his body, so that we would not have to, he paid it all.

I can remember years ago, (married, and not saved) I use to tell my girlfriends, I could really relate to Marvin Gaye's song, sexual healing, I felt that sex gave me peace, especially when I was really stressed out, I felt sex was what I needed to just relax the inner me, now even after I got divorced, I still had the same mind set, when I got saved and found out the truth, things changed in my life for the better, back then I told myself that God understood that I was a woman with needs, after all, he created me and he knew and understood that sex was just a part of my life.

Now I am telling you my testimony for a reason, not for you to talk about how foolish I was back then, I am showing you how my mind set was, and how God delivered me.

He delivered me, as my walk with him progressed, he was preparing me even back then.

God saved and delivered me from so many things, he even renewed my mind, by the hearing and believing of his word, I began to fall in love with the word, I craved, desiring to know more, I had never heard the truth, so it really felt like Christmas, I felt like a child getting something new, learning the truth will change you, from the inside out.

As I look back, I can remember the more word I received, the more I wanted to know, and before long more deliverance came, I was no longer bound, I began to even think differently.

I started to think about sex in a different way, I began to respect sex as a gift from God, not just a feeling to satisfy my flesh, I know it is a gift to married people, a gift between two people that have a covenant with the lord, that are joined together in holy matrimony, sex became sacred, it was not just a means of sexual fulfillment for my body or a way for me to show love to a man, it became sacred, during that time I received so much word, that the relationship I had with the lord began to deepen, I began hearing his voice more clearly.

I believed what the word of God said about my body and I began to live what the word said.

I knew my body was the temple of the living God, I began to respect myself, I had a desire to live a holy lifestyle, I wanted to be like him, the more word I heard, the more I received it in my heart, I began to change from the inside out. I became a doer of God's word, not just a hearer, my mind became renewed.

As time went on, I was tested on what I learned and believed in my heart, the enemy would put all kinds of thoughts in my mind about sex, and all kinds of feelings would come upon me. I had to learn to cast these thoughts and feelings down; I had to fight the good fight of faith, casting down all imaginations, that exalt itself against the knowledge of God, knowing that I was not fighting flesh and blood but wickedness in high places, the enemy was attaching my mind with former things from my past, I had to cast down these thoughts every time they surfaced in my mind.

We must not receive every thought, we must think on things that are pure and of a good report, read Philippians 4:8, think on what God has done, think on his finish work.

We must change our thought pattern; we must keep our minds on him, this is what keeps us in perfect peace. I had to meditate on the word of God more each day.

Philippians chapter two verse five says "Let this mind be in you, which was also in Christ Jesus."

It may seem hard to change our old pattern of thinking, but if we make a conscience effort, to hear and receive the word daily and began applying it to our everyday life, in doing so, we will change.

My motto is;

God will take you as you are, to become as he is.

It is not in the way we act when we see others looking at us, or the way we talk when we know that people are listening, it is our lifestyle, living holy, in our everyday living.

Most of us were not delivered from things over night, we must make a conscience effort to pray and seek God to help us to change. We cannot change on our own, but we can speed up the process by accepting the word in our hearts, not only hearing the word, but being doers of the word.

The Holy Spirit dwells in us; we are the very temple of the living God.

In 2 Corinthians 6:16 God said, "I will dwell in them, and walk in them; and I will be their God, and they shall be my people."

Practice makes perfect, keep reading the word of God, pray and meditate on the word daily, until it becomes your life, embedding inside your heart, remember we must have a desire to want to change.

2 Corinthians 5:17 tells us "Therefore if any man be in Christ, he is a new creature: old things are passed away; behold all things are become new."

Change will come when you have become more knowledgeable in the word of God, receiving the word for your life.

Remember in Hosea 4:6: "My people are destroyed for lack of knowledge"

To be knowledgeable of something, we must have a desire to want information and revelation on what we need to learn, we must have a desire in wanting to know him, learning through the holy spirit our best teacher, and learning by studying the word of God, also by the men and women that feed us the word.

We must not be unknowledgeable (ignorant)

To be ignorant is to be unaware, uninformed, and unknowingly, basically in the dark. The word of God gives us light and life.

God is love, when love comes into your heart you began to see yourself differently.

When I began to love myself, I realized how much the Lord loved and adored me, I saw myself differently, I began to see myself as he created me.

I can remember looking in the mirror one afternoon saying to myself what does God love about me.

Now of course I knew God so loved the world that he sent his only begotten son, but I still wanted to know why I was so special to him.

As I looked in the mirror, my eyes began to fill with tears, when he told me the plans, he had for my life, the more he revealed, the more I desired to go in the direction he was taking me, I didn't desire my will anymore, I only desired what he desired for my life, even though I did not understand fully what his plans were, I knew deep down in my heart, it was the only way for me to live.

I began to understand, when he died on the cross as a living sacrifice, he gave it all for me.

He laid down his life, to gain our life, he took it all, to give it all, and he gave the greatest gift of all, Himself.

Keeping our body for Jesus, is keeping our thought pattern in alignment with his word, meditating daily.

We must not receive (entertain) every thought (idea) that comes in our mind. When we receive certain thoughts, (beliefs) that are not of God, we bring to life that thought, we cause it to come into existence, especially when we speak (declare) what we are thinking.

Isaiah 26:3 says "Thou wilt keep him in perfect peace, whose mind is stayed on thee: because he trusteth in thee."

Every day we must speak the word of God over every situation we come up against, we must speak the word of God over our children, jobs, family, our neighborhoods, the government, mayor, president, co-workers and our church family, we must speak life at all times, and that life that we speak is the word God.

Stop trying to figure out everything in your life, just speak the truth, speak life and not death.

Speak (declare, say, utter) what God says, he can only perform, what we speak, and if we speak what the word of God says for our life, God can perform it in our lives, we must also be able to visualize, and believe what we speak.

If we speak what the devil says for our life, we are bringing to life what we speak, and he comes to steal, kill and destroy.

Speak positive confessions for your life and the life of others, be confident (certain and self-assured) in knowing what God has said, He is able (capable) to perform.

It is a blessing in obedience, being submissive to his authority.

Keeping our body for Jesus, is very rewarding and satisfying.

God's Ability Or Man's Ability

Ability is being able to have the capacity to do and perform successfully.

We believe him knowing, he cannot lie. We walk by faith and not by sight, living a lifestyle of trust in him, because he is our source.

In order to trust God, we must believe him at his word, knowing that it is already done, even before the foundations of the world were formed, we must believe the word of God without having any doubt, that if God said it, He is able to bring it to pass. God can not lie! Read Numbers 23:19.

We can't trust our human nature; we must trust God, without the evidence of seeing anything in the natural.

To trust is to have confidence in God, obeying what he says and having faith in his ability, he is responsible to care for us.

When we trust God, we have confidence in his ability, our faith and belief is in him, we depend on our Father totally, he is responsible for us, providing and caring for us.

I wrote a poem about what God has done in my life I would like to share it with you.

He will come

In the darkness of the night

His light will shine through

When pain is so unbearable

And doctors don't know what to do

Call the Master Physician Jesus, a healer

without a degree!

Rest he will come

When no one can help,

and your back is against the wall

When all is said and done, he will come

Look for him, seek and you will find,

My lord and savior

Believe me he will come

He who says he will come, will come and

not tarry

I would like to share this testament

I can remember at a time in my life while waiting on
the Lord to come through for me, I was robbing Peter
to pay Paul, paying bills on my credit card, and not
answering my phone, for fear of another bill collector
calling me, I had used up all my resources available,

no one could help me, what I needed only the lord could do.

I tried to believe God no matter how things looked, I was determined to walk by faith and not by sight, even though I couldn't see my way out.

I kept saying what God said about my situation, I looked up scriptures on what I needed to believe in my situation, I also began meditating and confessing each day. I told myself no matter how things appeared to be I would trust and believe God, well let me tell you, it seemed before things got better, they got worst.

At this time in my life, I began learning patience, and how to wait on the Lord.

Now believe me, I kept my confidence in the Lord and I didn't complain either, complaining only delays what God wants to do in your life, its causes unbelief and false confessions, go through your circumstances praising the lord, because, no matter how things look on the outside, God is not a man and he cannot lie, if God said it, he will come through for you, just believe him at his word!

One day while praying the Lord said to me, I am going to come through for you, my belief in God went to another level, I was at a total peace with what he had said, without visually seeing anything.

My confidence in God made me speak bold; I began to boast about what God was doing in my life, even before it manifest because I believed God.

When you believe God, you are not afraid to speak what he is saying and doing for you in life. You began to tell people even before its manifest, remember at times in your life, the lord will have you to keep silent before it manifest, because of their unbelief and doubt.

Well the rest is history; God came through like so many times before.

I am in love with him, and the more I learn about him, the more I love him, he captures every part of me.

In my whole life that I have lived, I can truly say with total honesty, I have never had a love like this before, he is laughter and tears of joy, I just love him with all I have within me.

We must not try to produce the blessings of God, by trying to make things happen, in our own ability. Time will determine if you want the Lord or just what he has to offer for your life, we must wait patiently on God, waiting long enough to see the manifestation of what he has said.

We must trust God's ability and not man's ability.

Faith comes by hearing and hearing by the word of God, there is no other way to get faith, except by hearing the word.

We can tell, when a person needs more word, when the storms of life come, they fall apart, not having enough word in their heart, they are not rooted and grounded.

God has a divine plan and purpose for our life, he already has an outline, a perfect plan, a divine layout of his, we are made for his purpose, to fulfill his plan in earth.

When you believe God at His word, your life changes, I am not saying you will not have any problems, trials or persecution in life, of course you will, but living holy along with knowing and trusting, believing and obeying God, will bring so much more peace, confidence and joy, no matter what you have to face in life.

God said I will never forsake or leave you; he is around at all times in our Christian walk, ready to help us in everything we encounter, and his willingness to comfort, lead and guide us from glory to glory is his desire.

You may be around many things in life, that are factual, but remember that God's word is truth, and truth over rides facts, that are present in your life.

Wait on the Lord and he shall renew your strength, stop trying in your own ability, and trust in God's ability.

Remember God's ability is able to do it, and has the capacity to perform successfully, with all power, for us to live victorious lives.

Keep Your Focus

To focus on something is to make a concentrated effort to keep your attention on a particular thing.

Staying focus means to keep our minds on Jesus; no matter how things look around us, we must remember everyday of our life, 2 Corinthians 5:7 "That we walk by faith and not by sight".

Having faith in God is to believe what he has already done before we see the manifestation of anything.

The enemy comes to take our attention off the word of God, he knows that if we are more concerned about all the problems and cares of this world we cannot concentrate on the things of God. Read 1Peter chapter five verse seven.

Walking by faith is kingdom living, walking by sight is walking only by what we can see in the natural.

What is the enemy putting in your mind or life as a distraction?

Sometimes, we just need to shut off the television, telephone and the video games, and concentrate on what the Lord is saying or performing for our life.

Take time out of your day to spend time with the lord, he wants to commune with us daily.

When we put God first, keeping our minds focus on him, our main emphasis will be on the word of God, of course we have other things in our daily lives, things like raising our children, caring for loved ones, cleaning our homes, cooking and a lot of other everyday life things that have to be taken care of, but our main focus will never stray away from God's word, for our everyday living, no matter what is taking place.

Keeping your focus is also renewing your mind, by what the word of God says.

Isaiah 26:3 says "Thou wilt keep him in perfect peace, whose mind is stayed on thee: because he trusteth in thee."

We must line up our thinking to what the word says about our life, each day speaking words of wisdom into our life and the life of others.

I can remember one day when the Lord told me not to turn on the television for the whole day, I really didn't mine because I don't watch much television, I love to read, so I never find much time to watch television, well I did just what God told me to do, and what a blessing it was, all that day the Lord revealed some awesome things, revealing not only about my life, but the lives of other people, now just think if I didn't obey him, not turning off the television, I would have missed instructions, and a lot of insight into my life and the lives of others, remember it is a blessing when you obey the voice of the Lord. Read Jeremiah 7:23 and Acts 5:29

Stop letting the devil talk you out of what God has revealed for you to do. A lot of times we talk ourselves out of obeying God, by questioning what he has said, asking ourselves is this really God that I'm hearing or is it just me? When this happens, the Lord always says to me, you know my voice.

John chapter ten verse twenty-seven says, "My sheep hear my voice, and I know them, and they follow me."

When you have a relationship with the Lord you spend time in prayer, the more time you spend with him, the more you know him, the more he reveals to you, the more he can trust you.

One day while praying God said to me, our intimate time is between us, well I began to question the Lord, asking him what exactly did he mean by this, he said our time together is very intimate and private, he began to also explain to me that a husband and wife, never expose, what goes on in the bedroom, it's their personal intimate time together, not to be a topic of conversation with no one, and this is what he wanted me to see, about our relationship.

God began to bring back to my remembrance, of how many times out of excitement, I would run to the phone, call up friends or people I felt close to, I began to reveal to them about all the intimate time I spent with God, and everything he said, I soon began to understand, that what the lord revealed was for me personally and not everyone, I soon learned how to operate and function in the things he trusted to reveal.

I also notice that different times in life, when I couldn't keep my focus, was because some things I should have kept secret instead of confiding in others, some did not have the faith to believe God, they began to sow seeds of doubt in my heart, everyone that is around you, doesn't have the faith to believe what God has shown you for your life, these people were not necessarily my enemies, they just could not believe what I was believing, they had a limit on God, and I didn't.

Everybody that is around you is not necessary for you, sometimes they are against you, sent for that very purpose in your life to keep you unfocused, anytime a person is keeping strife, confusion or anger in your life, even carnal things, you need to take inventory of your relationship with that person, especially if they consistently bring up your past.

Stay focus on his word, and the plans he has for your life, do not lose your confidence in God, you are here for a purpose, and that purpose is to do his will.

To stay focus is to trust the word of God, to accept in our mind that the word of the living God is true and real, we honor Gods word, by letting it lead and guide us, trusting him with everything in our lives, our children, jobs, finances, health even our friends, we trust him with our entire life. He is the landlord and keeper of our life.

When you trust God for your life, you include him on every decision you make, regardless of how large or small.

We focus on what he has said, knowing that he has the answers we need. Pray and trust his answer, it may be yes or even no, he may be telling you to just wait and stand still, whatever he says just do it!

Staying focus is meditating on the word daily, not only when you need a quick fix.

The enemy comes to steal, kill and destroy, the word of God for your life.

To steal is to take unlawfully something that belongs to someone else, to take illegally without the permission of another, is a thief, to kill is to slaughter murder, ruin or block a plan, to overpower or slay, to destroy is to demolish, tear down, damage or overthrow.

These are the things the enemy tries to attempt in our lives, this is why we have to stay focus, keeping the word in our hearts and mind, to stay focus keeps us on the right path, to the right way of living.

When we stay focus on the word of God for our lives, we don't get side tracked by the carnality of things in the world or people, we will stay in remembrance of who we are, and why we are living a holy lifestyle, for the Lord.

People are observing our lives to see if we are real or just mouth service. Are you living a holy lifestyle, when no one is looking?

These are things that will keep us focus, that we must do daily.

1. Hearing and reading the word of God, faith comes by hearing and hearing by the word of God. We must read and study the word for ourselves.

2. Praying

    We must communicate with God, spending time alone with him.

3. Meditating on the word of God.

    We must ponder on the word in our heart, concentrating on the word.

4. Believe the word

    We must accept the word, knowing and believing the word of God is true and real.

5. Confessing the word

    We must declare the word of God; it speaks life into us and others.

6. Living Holy

When we live a godly lifestyle, we pattern our life after Jesus.

7. Loving the lord and loving people

   When we love the Lord, we are acknowledging him as first in our life, we have no other gods before him, and we are caring and concerned about the wellness of others.

8. Obeying God

   We must submit to God, yielding and surrendering to his will for our life.

We Are the Light of the World

Matthew 5:16 says "Let your light so shine before men, that they may see your good works and glorify your Father which is in heaven."

We are the light of this world, our brightness, glow, and radiance, give light into a world of darkness, we stand out by the lifestyle we live.

Our lifestyle should draw people to Jesus, they are watching our every move, observing to see if the words we speak, are lining up with the way we are truly living.

People are tired of imaginary, artificial and traditional people that go to church every Sunday and are living for the devil trying to look holy to the world.

People are observing your life, every day they need to see that you don't go to those places anymore, or listen to that kind of music or watch that certain thing on the television, they need to hear that your conversation has changed, from cursing, gossiping and talking against people, they need to see it is no longer a part of your life.

They need to see a real person, that loves the lord and is willing to lay down their life to show others the goodness of God, and how he is manifested in our life, that we not only talk that talk, but we are walking the walk that so many desire to see.

How can we expect the world to want what we have, when we can only offer them what they already have?

We must let our light so shine, that people will ask and seek to find out what they must do to be saved.

We are that, brightness they see in the world; we are that glow.

I can remember a sister in the ministry I attended, smiling at me, she finally approached me asking if I was getting married?

I responded by asking her why she ask me that question, she said I had such a glow on my face, I look so content and full of joy, I told her it was the joy of the lord and I also told her, yes I am getting married, I just haven't met him yet.

She saw that light in me and she saw that light on me, the light of the lord.

We should smile more as Christians, yes we all go through, but how are we to draw others to Christ if we look sad or mean all the time, we really do have so much to be thankful for, no matter what we are going through, God is there to lead and comfort and help in the time of our need, remember the battle has already been won!

I smile because I am content, at rest and joyful, I choose to believe God and no matter what is going on in my life, I choose to stand on the word of God, the word makes us confident in knowing, that the God we serve is able to do all things!

We must stop pretending to be what we want people to perceive us to be. Never let anyone call you out of your character, it's your distinctive quality of who God made you to be, we must never pretend to be something that we are not.

To pretend is to make something seem to be true, or to act in a way intended to make people believe something untrue or misleading, giving a false impression, being a deceiver.

We need to be our authentic self, when we try to do things that are not ordained for our life, we will not operate on a fullness of what we are pursuing to accomplish.

We are not to try to fulfill another person's destiny, they are anointed to do what the lord called them to do, staying in our path in which we are called, will produce what God has already placed inside of us, for that very purpose.

When people see that we are not the real McCoy, it's a turn off, we must stop making false impressions, deceiving people.

We are also to demonstrate a Christian lifestyle, not only when we are in the lord's house, or in front of the preacher or in the presence of church members.

Are you living a lifestyle for Jesus?

God is doing a new thing in the earth, old things are passed away, he is using people that are authentic, real people we would least expect to be used.

People who don't know how to be fake, common people without a degree, without a reputation, he's saving and delivering that alcoholic you turned your nose up at, or that prostitute, even that person on drugs, you felt you couldn't minister to, because they didn't look or act like you, the most unlikely people will be used in the kingdom of God, he's raising up people, that will say yes lord, use me, it's a new season, it is time to stop playing church, and be the church, people so desperately need.

Read Romans 8:19.

We are the light of the world and it's time to shine.

God desires sons and daughters, to step up to the plate and take our place as kings and priests in this world, speaking and demonstrating our power and authority, having no lack in our lives, living abundantly, lending and not borrowing, healing the sick, raising the dead, laying hands on blind eyes to see, we are the head not the tail, above only and not beneath, yes that time is now, and we need to wake up and stop pretending to be what we are not, and become who God says we are.

It is time to be a light for those that are loss, to grow up and walk in your destiny, taking your place in God's divine plan.

It is time for those rivers of living water to come up and out of your belly into others.

We must tap into what God is doing in our life, and line up with the word of God, hearing as well as being a doer of the word.

Don't be loss, appearing to be holy and righteous, we must keep a close relationship with the lord; walking by faith and not by sight.

I had to ask myself some serious questions, we all have to examine ourselves, what does my character say about me? Can the world see Jesus in me? When people come in my presence, after they leave, how do they feel, drained or lifted up? Have you ever asked yourself these questions?

When I pray, I ask the lord what it is he wants to show me about myself, that I have a deaf ear to, many times in life, the lord is showing us things about ourselves, and we plug our spiritual ears, not hearing his voice, because we really do not desire to change in certain areas of our life.

God is calling us to be what we are predestinate to be in this earth, either the devil is your father or God is your father, even in the natural, a child cannot have two biological fathers.

The time is now, we must be about our father's business, letting our light shine in a world of darkness.

We must be obedient to everything the lord is telling us to do, we are living in the last days, and we must shine to bring people out of darkness, praying, interceding for souls, meditating on the word of God, we must never pass people by thinking someone else is going to tell them about Jesus, why do you think you have so much word inside, It is for the saving, deliverance and healing of souls.

I can remember years ago, I was a babe in Christ, I told the lord I had a desire to tell people about him, I just didn't know how.

One day while inside a takeout food place, I saw this woman whose face look familiar, I smiled at her and the lord said to me, tell her about me, I told the lord, I did not know how to just start a conversation with this woman, he told me to speak to her and he would do the rest, so I spoke and told her my name, and began to tell her what God put on my heart to say, that if I found a buried treasure in my back yard and it was more than enough for me, I would share with my family and friends, and help all the people that I could, then I told her, that I had found something that changed my life, gave me peace, healed my body and gave me joy, and I would naturally like to share this treasure with her, and that this treasure was Jesus.

I told her I really didn't want to take up her time, but he was so good to me and had changed my life in so many different ways, I wanted everyone to know him. She asked me what church I attended and a few more questions, the rest is history, the lord saved her.

God had me tell this story to so many people, some people gave their life to Jesus as I ministered to them, and I know that others are on the way, you see I did what God told me to do, the seed was planted in their heart and some one else will come along and water that seed.

The more God had me to approach people, the easier it became, I love telling people about Jesus, sometimes the lord will have you tell them your personal testimony that is similar to their life, or he may reveal something about them.

Wherever you are, in your walk with the lord, do not be discouraged, let God prepare you for purpose, always know that he will use you just where you are, and as you grow, he can trust you with more of what he has plan for your life.

Think of it this way, would you buy an infant baby a bike? Of course not, an infant hasn't even learned how to crawl yet. Preparation is before manifestation.

We are the light of the world and we shine; we must love; it is in our loving that our hearts are changed into becoming more like the lord.

The Wages of Sin Is Death

2 Corinthians 5:21 "For he hath made him to be sin for us, who knew no sin that we might be made the righteousness of God in him."

Spiritual death is separation from God, natural death is the ending of all vital functions in your body, you are without life.

The wages of sin is death. The word wage means your just reward or recompense for something. We can really say that the reward of continually sinning, without repentance is death, it is a person's just reward for the things they have sown in their everyday life, you reap what you sow.

To reap means, you will receive what you have sown, the fruits of your labor. If you sow to the flesh you will reap corruption.

I can remember a story told to me about the painting of the Lords supper, it has been quite a while since I've told this story to anyone, so if you know the story and I haven't explained it the right way please forgive me, I'm almost sure the story is real, I like for you to see the moral meaning of the story.

One day a man was painting the Lords supper, and he saw a man's face that he wanted to use in his painting as the face of Jesus, he asked the man and he agreed to let him use his face in the painting, he was a Christian man and I imagine his face had a gentle, soft, appearance, all the things we would imagine Jesus would have looked like, well as I can remember this painting of the Lords supper, took years to complete, so each character he needed for his painting, probably took years for the painter to find, making sure he had the right face to portray each character.

Well at last he needed a person's face to paint for Judas, he found a man that was perfect, he had a look of a betrayer, just as he imagine Judas might have looked, and the painter approached him explaining to him, about how he was almost finished with this painting and all he needed was a face portraying Judas Iscariot, the man that betrayed Jesus for thirty pieces of silver.

The man he approached was so surprised, because years earlier his face was portrayed as Jesus, and now he wanted to use his face as Judas in the painting.

I may not have the correct information about the story, but if you notice how much this man's facial appearance had changed, just from the sin that was in his life, how he went from being saved and set free having a gentle soft, kindhearted face, the same man must have went back into the world, living in sin and unbelief, even wickedness, and how this drastically changed his outward appearance from that of Jesus to the appearance of Judas, his face must of looked worn, unpleasant even wicked.

It is amazing, how the painter used the same man for both characters, the face of Jesus and the face of Judas.

Sin is real, look how it even changes our facial appearance, we are changed from the inside out, so in other words, what is on the inside will manifest on the outside eventually, if you keep it in you long enough.

I can remember at certain times in my life, I have looked at people and seen the light of the lord on their faces, like a glow, a radiance about them that only God can give, they had a peacefulness, a restful appearance.

When we die spiritually, we are separated from God, we no longer have that closeness to the Lord, we can no longer hear his voice, when we don't have a relationship with him, we are not being led by the holy spirit and we won't know his will for our life, we no longer live a life of abundance, peace joy or righteousness, we are no longer in the kingdom of God, sin takes us away from God, sin is unbelief.

The wages of sin is death, it is death to our health our finances, peace and joy, death slowly gets inside of every part of our life and it destroys and kills everything that prospers on the inside and out.

Sin destroys what God has accomplished for our life; it brings death to everything living in us, it also brings death to the word of God, stealing our very destiny God has planned for our lives.

We must know the word of truth, because the truth sets us free. Take this thought for your life today, God is life, sin is death.

When our character resembles the world, people can't be drawn to the lord, and we may be the only light they will ever see, we must live a life set apart from the world, living holy, because he is holy, our character is to be the character of Jesus and not the character of the world.

As Christians our character has the distinctive qualities of Jesus, we have his nature and behavior, our essential character is like his, and this changes our personality to having a character of uprightness in our everyday living, having a defining character as the Lord we no longer live in sin.

God is our entirety.

The lord is our everything, our entirety, from beginning to end, he is complete, he is everything that is needed for our lives.

God is everywhere, no matter where you are, he is there, he is our source for living, never running dry, he is living waters, our caretaker, he is concern about every part of our life. He is our protector, keeping us out of harm's way, and warning us of things to come, he is our supplier that supplies all of our needs, and gives us the desires of our heart.

He says in his word that if we seek first the kingdom of God, and all his righteousness, all these other things shall be added, and that is everything we need. He assures us of his promises, that what he says, he is also able and willing to perform.

He is a healer, maintaining our physical and mental wellbeing, manifesting his word in our bodies, he is our peace, our joy, pleasure and delight, our light in a world of darkness, our hope when all has become depleted, he is the great I Am! The greatest lover we have ever known.

Gossiping

To gossip is to be a habitual talker, someone given to spreading personal or intimate information about other people. Spreading rumors is about the same definition as gossip, rumors are to tell personal or intimate facts about other people, sometimes maliciously.

A rumor is always an unverified report, a general circulated story, or statement without facts to confirm the truth.

How does gossip effects the body of Christ?

It destroys the body of Christ, reducing us to perform at our fullest capability.

It defeats the body Of Christ, causing failure for us to be on one accord.

It uproots the body of Christ, it damages, displaces and destroys completely.

The enemy is always accusing and blaming us before the Lord, so when we gossip, we are giving the devil (the accuser) ammunition, to accuse the body of Christ before the Lord.

Gossip destroys people, sometimes so severely the damage it leaves behind has to be restored and repaired, because it wrecks the lives of others, the danger it causes is very harmful.

I must mention my own testimony about how the Lord dealt with me about gossip.

I began to fellowship with a couple of sisters, we began to go out to dinner quite frequently, I noticed there conversation always leaned towards other people's personal or private lives, after a while, spending time with them on a regular basis, I began to talk about what I knew about people, before long I began repeating everything I thought I knew about other people's lives, I noticed each time after spending time with them, I would go home feeling drained and guilty.

1Corinthians chapter fifteen verse thirty- three says;

"Be not deceived: evil communications corrupt good manners."

One night while praying the Lord said to me, why are you talking about my body? I began to tell the lord I am your body, the lord said, I was gossiping and tattling about the body of Christ, this scared me so bad I didn't say anything else about anyone. I realized I was not going to be around people that gossiped because it made me feel to uncomfortable and guilty, each time I left these sisters after having dinner I'd go home feeling drained.

Well the rest is history, I had to stop fellowshipping with them, of course I loved them, but God was removing me from corrupt communication.

Gossip never builds up a person, it never edifies or exhorts, gossip only destroys, it even creates lies.

One person can tell a story about another person, and it may be true, but by the time the story about that person gets to the fifth or sixth person, it has become a different story altogether, different than when it first started, this is the reason why we need to be very careful about what we repeat to others.

When a person shows us another person's faults, we are to pray for them and keep our mouths off of them.

Ask yourself this question, what am I talking about every day?

We all need to take inventory of ourselves, I had to take a look at myself, and when I did, I didn't like what I saw, so I changed it, I never stop trying, it is a daily walk.

When we are loving each other, we speak life and encouraging uplifting words.

Loving is a commandment. Read Matthew 22:37-39.

True love is not only mouth service, it is demonstrating brotherly and sisterly compassion towards one another.

Gossip kills, love and the word of God heals.

Loving the Hurt Away

I want to talk to you about a subject that is not very popular, nor is it easy to talk about, most people really do not know how to deal with the hurts and wounds of others, they simply tell them, God will work it out, or trouble does not last always!

Well, sometimes troubles last too long, and nothing is working out.

The enemy sends things to discourage us, but we must remember, somethings in life that we go through, are lessons we need to grow and mature in, to become the sons and daughters of God, and he will get your attention in certain situations. I could go on and on about why bad things happen in our lives or why trouble seems to always last too long, but one thing I am sure of, God is always on time, we must pray, casting all your burdens on the Lord, he cares for us.

We must take inventory of ourselves, not only when we think we should, or because things are simply not working out on our behalf.

God wants to bless us abundantly, he loves us so much, he is just waiting for us to grow up, and become the sons and daughters, he has predestinated us to be, so we can live kingdom living, a lot of us still do not get it, we are still disobeying the Lord and wondering why things are not happening on our behalf, only you can stop your blessings, remember, we must obey God at all times.

To obey is to follow instruction, to do as you are told to do, following is to be led, we must obey and be led by God.

Delayed obedience is disobedience, it is struggling in your mind, whether you will agree and obey with what God is telling you to do.

We often do this when we do not believe God and the word that is being preached.

Disobedience means to refuse to obey instruction or authority, you are in opposition with God, you are in conflict with what he is instructing you to do.

When we do not obey God, we are in total disagreement of what his plans are for our life, remember to lean not to your own understanding, and in all your ways acknowledging him and he will direct your path. When we choose our own direction, we get in the way of God's instruction and plans for our life.

Getting back to the subject loving the hurt away, we must love people until the hurt is gone, this means to pray for them, speak positive confessions in their life, we are to show compassion, love and understanding, we are to edify the body, reassuring them of the goodness of God.

Sometimes we must give our very own testimony, bearing witness to what they are going through, telling them how at one time in our lives, we felt just as helpless and afraid as they have felt, and how we became confident in our walk with God.

Faith comes by hearing and hearing by the word of God. (Romans 10:17)

When we love people, we show tender affection, kindness and compassion towards that person, we appreciate who they are, and we are concerned about the well-being of that person, loving a person is to lend a helping hand.

Being a good listener sometimes is all a person needs, just a listening ear, also remember to take their burden to the lord, the one that can change things.

I have found in my own life experiences, that at times it is very hard to love some people, I try to put myself in that persons place, but we understand that we can't always have the answers as to why people do certain things, we must love them regardless of the way they act, we can show love to that person by ministering the word of God and praying for them.

We must love the unlovable, not being concern about their appearance, just love them beyond there faults.

God is love, and we are to be as he is in this earth, when we represent the lord, we represent love, and whatever we do, we must do it in love.

Read 1John 4:8.

Loving is not always giving money or stepping in to rescue a person, God may want that person to trust in him only.

Sometimes things are taken away from a person, so they can depend on God, he will take away all their props, even shoulder they cry on.

God desires to be the only one that we depend on for everything, learning to trust him for all our needs, not depending on man. Read Psalm 118:8.

The Lord will give you wisdom and knowledge on how to proceed in the decisions you make, or he will do a miracle, maybe even send people to help, but he wants you to put all your trust in him.

You must not handicap a person to a point, where they trust what you can do more than what God can do, you can become the god of their life, they began to trust only you for that particular thing, when God wants them to trust him only.

As parents we sometimes jump in, when God wants us to stand back and watch his glory in our children's life, at times in my own life God has told me to take my hands off of the situation in my children's life and to just pray, because sometimes you are doing more harm than good, so the next time you see a need before stepping in, pray and let the Lord lead you on what you should or should not do in a person's life, because many times we come to a person's rescue, and the lord wants us to step back and let him have his way in their life.

I am a parent, and I love my children, but I also know that when the lord tells me to take my hands off, I have to be obedient to what he is doing.

Sometimes it is not a pretty sight, but God chastens those who he loves, and believe me, he loves our children just as he loves us.

It is very hard to visually see your child being chastened by the Lord, but know this one thing, if you get in the way, progress can never be made on their behalf.

It is good that God sends people in our lives to help alone the way to our destiny, but we must remember, we can never make people our main source, we only have one main source to depend on and that source is Jesus, he is lord over our lives, our very foundation, our benefit that supplies everything we need.

Life of Abundance

"The thief cometh not, but for to steal, and to kill, and to destroy, I am come that they might have life, and that they might have it more abundantly." John 10:10.

"Now unto him that is able to do exceeding abundantly above all that we ask or think, according to the power that worketh in us." (Ephesians 3:20)

To live in abundance, we must know God's will for our life, it states in Ephesians 5:17, "Wherefore be ye not unwise, but understand what the will of the Lord is."

God blesses us to have a life of abundance, a life of overflow, flooding over with everything we need, not only for ourselves, but for others.

An abundant life is having a surplus in an amount that exceeds the limit of fullness, complete with nothing missing, you are living in a wealthy place, having more than enough, lacking no good thing.

Psalm 34:10 says, "The young lions do lack and suffer hunger: but they that seek the Lord shall not want any good thing."

Psalms chapter thirty-seven and verse four says; "Delight thyself also in the Lord; and he shall give thee the desires of thine heart."

God is not talking about a typical or average way of living, he is speaking of a lifestyle that is complete, nothing missing, a lifestyle in abundant health, safety, provisions, miracles, blessings and favor, abundance living is so much more than just money.

Obedience brings on the blessings.

"Behold to obey is better than sacrifice.' 1 Samuel 15:22.

In order to live and have an abundant way of life, we must obey the lord.

Job 36:11 states that "If they obey and serve him, they shall spend their days in prosperity, and their years in pleasure."

Obeying God is to follow his instructions, submitting to his authority, we must be in total agreement with the word of God, remember delayed obedience, is disobedience.

When you disobey, you go against his word, when you refuse to do as he says, you are willfully disrespecting and rebelling against his authority.

Isaiah 1:19 says: "If ye be willing and obedient ye shall eat the good of the land."

Matthew 6:33 states, that if we seek the kingdom of God and all his righteousness first all these other things will be added to us.

Seeking after the kingdom of God, is to find and strive towards him and all his righteousness, we must go after him, seeking revelation, and understanding of his character, and his will, for life.

Seek things that cannot corrupt, rust or rot, we must seek after the kingdom of God and all his righteousness, to obtain wisdom, knowledge and understanding, having a desired relationship with him.

It is a good to have material possessions, but we must not have our main emphasis on material gain, God desires for us to live a life of abundance, but in all that we obtain, we must love and seek him first.

For many years people thought that the church was supposed to be happy, shouting and broke, they were told that money was the root to all evil, and if you had to much you would go straight to hell.

This is a lie, the lord desires to prosper his children, that our joy may be full. 1Timothy 6:10 says; "For the love of money is the root of all evil: which while some coveted after, they have erred from the faith, and pierced themselves through with many sorrows."

It says in this verse, for the love of money, that means you are placing money above other things, this makes it the root of all evil.

We are the children, of the Highest God, my father owns it all. Knowing and believing what the lord has said, keeps joy and peace in our heart, and what he has said will surely come to pass, he cannot lie.

In Isaiah chapter fifty five and verse eleven it says, "So shall my word be that goeth forth out of my mouth: it shall not return unto me void, but it shall accomplish that which I please, and it shall prosper in the thing whereto I sent it."

This is not an easy subject to discuss, but this very thing happen in my life and I am almost sure it has taken place in the lives of others.

The enemy comes to take unlawfully what belongs to us. One particular way he does this is through trickery and deception, to mislead us, destroying the word within.

The enemy will use whomever he will to come against you, just as the lord sends people to assist us on our journey, the devil sends people to hinder or destroy what God has plan for us, remember he comes to steal, kill and destroy, but God says, I give you life, and a life of abundance.

We are not fighting against flesh and blood, but against spiritual wickedness in high places.

The enemy desires to destroy your life, he is desperately trying to get us to have a spiritual abortion, to abort what the lord has ordained for us, even before you were in your mother's womb.

Some people are such great pretenders, observing your every move, perceiving to be someone that they are really not, sooner or later you will know them by the fruit they bare. They are sent to keep you distracted and unfocused.

The enemy wants you to miscarriage your destiny, to have a cancellation on all the plans to your destination God has set for you. Most times that devil tries to work through people around us, even our family members, to try to terminate our future.

Now we all know that no weapon formed against us can prosper, it can form, but it will never prosper in our life, no one can stop what the lord has plan for our life, our disobedience and unbelief can delay things, pushing us back, going around in the same circle again, we must repent and turn around, he is faithful to forgive us and place us back on our journey he has planned.

We must love people and keep them in prayer, but we must not let those negative, unbelieving, self-righteous, abortionists, that are sent by the devil to delay, hinder or abort what God is accomplishing in our lives, and I don't care how well they quote the bible or how well they pray, they speak well with their mouth, but the insecurities of their mind, has them wavering in unbelief, be led by the Holy Spirit on who you let into your life, of course we are here to minister to people that don't know the lord, but as mama used to say, just because the donkey talked doesn't mean you need to take him home.

We must even use wisdom in asking someone to agree with us in prayer, if we take the time out to acknowledge the lord, by asking him who we should let be in agreement with us in prayer, instead of us picking who we feel is more spiritual, you could be doing yourself more harm than good. The devil tries to appear as an angel of light to deceive us.

We are predestinated, God has determined our outcome beforehand, so we are in preparation before the manifestation of the plans he has for our life.

The Lord is blessing us, and the world is waiting for the manifestation of the sons of God. Read Romans chapter eight and verse nineteen.

We are the body, sent for the purpose of doing the will of God in the earth.

The most important relationship you will ever have is your relationship with him, he is Lord over all, and as I specified before, the more time you spend with him, the more you will know his voice.

Why are women so desperate to get married?

To be desperate is to be overwhelm with urgency, frantic, anxious, worried and distressed, to be desperate is also to become eager and impatience.

A lot of women think if they can get married, everything will become perfect, this is a fantasy you have created in your imagination, a pipe dream, as my mama use to say.

Some women perceive that obtaining a husband, is every poor girl's dream, and every rich girl's prayer, I believe it use to be a song similar to that back in the day.

I have had plenty of conversations with sisters, expressing the reason they desire to have a husband, let me share more than a few reasons; I want to be loved, appreciated, treasured and cherished, respected, admired, taken care of, and last but not least, I want security and a good sexual relationship.

Single women of God, I love you and I understand, what I'm about to share with you does not relate to all single women, I pray you still love me when the sister to sister talk is finished.

We want a fantasy marriage with all the benefits of a superman, that can do it all!

We are in panic mode, and we feel that the Lord needs to manifest that husband now.

Sister to Sister

I am getting older, I have never been married before, I have been divorced for so long, and I want to still be able to _____, (you fill in the blank) and I am so lonely.

Let me first address the issue of getting older.

Look at Sara, now I know when Sara (Abraham's wife) got pregnant by her husband, they had to make love in order for her to bring forth a child, and I can imagine she must have enjoyed her husband, they had to make love to produce, you will not lose what you are not using, God can restore everything, just as he did with Abraham and Sara.

Age has nothing to do with how well you will enjoy life, or the things God has for you, including a husband. It is said in Genesis the twenty- first chapter verse two, that Sara conceived and bare Abraham a son in his old age, at the set time God had spoken to him.

Listen carefully, the set time, God did not do it until the set time.

It's your set time.

If you are an older woman, take a look at yourself, you are refined, polished, and have experienced a few things in life, you've been through some storms, and now you can handle some things, you have a mature mind, you have been strengthen, settled and of moral integrity, able to satisfy the husband God gives to you.

It's time for you to be celebrated!

How can we ask the lord for something, we are not willing to become ourselves?

For instance, you make a request to the lord desiring to have a man that is in love with you, ask yourself this question do you have a close relationship with the lord? And what about, lord I want a man that takes care of me, who is taking care of you now, I hope it's the lord.

The other most often thing I hear is, I have never been married before.

Sisters look back over your life, at that brother you thought you were in love with, and maybe you were, what if you married him, can you honestly say that you would still be married today,

I talked to my girlfriend the other day and she said to me, I've never been married before and I'm getting older, she even stated that if the lord blessed me with another husband before she got married, it would be unfair, I told my sister friend, if she knew all the things I endured and suffered through, in my marriage, she would count it a blessing to not have gone through, the things I went through, sometimes the lord spares us from what others have went through, so count it all joy.

Another subject I have discussed with women is they desire to be able to _____, You fill in the blank. Once you know how, like riding a bike, you never forget how to do whatever you are concerned about, God can restore, resurrect, and replenish what you need.

Is anything too hard for God, if the dear lord had you wait this long, there must be a reason why, look on the positive side, when the lord has his hands on your situation, it is well done, and his timing is perfect. His ways are not our ways nor is his timing or seasons in our times, preparation is before manifestation.

This should have been at the top of the list of concerns, I am so lonely.

I had to actually look up the definition of the word lonely, just to understand the meaning of what they were feeling.

Lonely means; to feel alone, sadden, isolated, lacking companionship, feeling secluded, without enough social contact.

I prayed to the lord about loneliness, because I do not feel lonely. Now when I did not have the lord in my life and I needed deliverance in different areas of my life, I felt lonely, I had different desires and a different lifestyle all together.

Why are so many Christian women lonely?

They do not have a relationship with the Lord.

When you have a relationship with the lord, you do not have time to be lonely, and if you find yourself lonely, it's because you are not spending enough time with the lover of your soul.

Having a relationship with God, is having a connection, you spend time alone with him, meditating and communicating, your thoughts began to line up with the plans he has for your life. You began to have the heart of his desires.

We fall in love with the lord, having a great desire to please him, not only with lip service, but also in our everyday walk, seeking his will to be done in our life.

We must rest and abide in his love; he is the greatest lover of all. You will never feel alone or lonely because he is always there.

He will never leave or forsake you, now remember, God cannot lie, so fall in love with him, put the lord first and all these other things (a husband) will come.

A lot of times what we desire to have, is not what the lord desires for us, we must seek God to see, if it is his will for us to marry, or just our desire.

What is a number ten?

Some would say a perfect ten, is a Mr. fine well dressed, big bank account, Mercedes, Lexus or Bentley driving brother, alone with the live-in mansion. What you see is not always what you get, like my mama use to say, what looks good is not always good for you.

Well let's get back to the real world.

A number ten is what God gives, that is tailor made just for you, it is a custom fit, perfectly suited only for you.

What you see is not always what you get, he can be a almond, chocolate, dark brown, white or chestnut colored brother, whatever you desire, he might have a big bank account with all the trimmings to go alone with it, but beware, he might have a body by Fisher (Fisher use to be the name of a car company) and a mind by Mattel. (Mattel made toys)

Most women and men seeking a number ten, are looking for a fantasy, I am not telling you to settle for less in a person, just be realistic and know the difference from real or imaginary.

Money, Sex and Power

We must stop prostituting our looks, checkbook, or body, to lure a brother or sister. Where did we get the notion that a candy man or woman, (giving gifts, sex, favors, money) will get you the person of your dreams, your body is not a taste test, nor are your lips a kissing contest!

Read 1Corinthians chapter six, verse nineteen.

Luring a person with the big three, sex, money and power, won't last, because before long another person will come along with more money then you have to offer, greater sex and more power, now I know there is not any grounded stable in love with the lord, Christian singles out their living as the world lives. We must recognize that we are sons and daughters of the highest God, and we do not operate in the world system, we are kingdom minded, living as kings and priests in this world.

Love where you are in your walk with the lord, in our journey we must not complain or murmur, this leads to having no peace, or any satisfaction in our path to our destiny, we must be content, enjoying the freedom of pursuing some of the things that we now have the time for, who knows maybe later when we are married, we may not have a lot of free time for ourselves, we are to relish each moment of what the lord has for our life right now.

We will not enjoy today, when we are living and waiting on every tomorrow to make us happy and content.

I can remember asking my pastor years earlier, did he think I would ever marry? Now that I think about it, what a stupid question, I noticed he took a long look in my direction and said, when you get a desire to have a husband, you will have one, I think deep in my heart he knew, I had no desire to be married at that particular time in my life.

God had to actually change my desires, I could not even visualize the idea of getting married, I did not desire any part of my life living with another man, and if you met me after my divorce, you would of thought I belonged to, The man Hater club of America.

The lord had to heal me, I had become very bitter, and blinded by unforgiveness. I can remember one day having a conversation with this brother at the church I attended, somehow we began discussing what I thought about men or something pertaining to men, I realize I said some terrible things about men, this brother had to have the love of God in his heart, he told me he was going to pray for me, because I needed help and deliverance, of course I began telling him that I was only speaking the truth, well of course the only truth I knew.

Eventually my healing and deliverance came, I thank that brother for his prayers. I had to forgive and stop blaming other for the hurt I felt. I began receiving in my heart wisdom and understanding on forgiveness, and how I must leave the past behind in order to move forward, only in letting go of my past, could I take hold of my future, that was predestinated for my life from the beginning.

We must permit ourselves to go forward and leave our past behind.

Single women, daughters of the highest God, live each day satisfied with the blueprint the lord has for your life. Stay in faith, rest, knowing he is everything you need him to be, slumber in the shelter of his protection, be still, your heart is well cultivated in his holy word, remember your destiny is in his hands.

Confess this for your life: I personalized this verse for myself, Romans 4:20-21. I staggered not at the promises of God through unbelief, but I am strong in faith, giving glory to God, I am fully persuaded, that what God has promised me, he is also able to perform.

The lord has a blueprint for each of our lives, a plan that is tailor made just for you. Enjoy your life, along your way to your destiny, living in the fullness of each day.

His plan exceeds anything we could even imagine for our life.

There have been times in my life, where I didn't know how I was going to make it through, I had come to a point in my life where no one could help me, not only was my back up against a wall, I didn't have a wall to lean on, no one could help me out of my dilemma, a lot of people I loved turned their backs on me, kinship meant nothing and friendship had no existence.

At this time in my life, before the lord rescued my body, mind and soul, I attempted suicide, I thought my life wasn't worth the drink I had in my hand, occasionally smoking marijuana seemed to relax my ability to live in a real world, facing real problems, and liquor became the drowning of sorrows in my life.

I was married almost twenty years, a blessing of two children came out of this union, I won't get deep into why the relationship ended, but it had such an astounding effect on my heart, and mind, even after

God healed me, I still practiced the hurt, not knowing how to begin a new life.

I have gone through ups and downs, emptiness, highs and lows, I've been raped, and wounded, discouraged and bewildered and almost loss my mind, but through it all, the lord led me out, he kept me, even when I thought he was not there. I came to the realization, all I had was him. At the lowest point in my life, his hands and arms were open, waiting for me to take my place.

Nothing will separate me from his love, mercy, kindness and grace, that surrounds me like a covering over my very soul. It is a divine pleasure to know him, and to learn of him.

Even in my sin, he loved me, at times I feel his breath, his touch, he is present, when I slumber and sleep, he is forever near, I appreciate how much pleasure, happiness, joy and peace he has given, his love makes me feel pretty, my whole being is content, he causes me to be at ease singing a song of laughter in my heart.

Jesus causes me to rest in the assurance of who he is, forsaking all to gain all that he has for my life.

"Seek ye first the kingdom of God, and his righteousness; and all these things shall be added unto you."

All these things are everything you will ever need.

The only way we can operate in the kingdom of God effectively, is to forsake the world. Love good and hate evil, love righteousness and hate sin.

Forsake is to give up something, to renounce or desert it, leaving it alone, to reject or remove yourself from it, abandoning and withdrawing from all ungodliness and unrighteousness.

As Christians we have a desire to operate in kingdom living, but until we make a conscience effort to forsake the things of the world, we will keep going around that same mountain, never to reach our full potential or live in the destiny God predestinated.

What does it mean to forsake the world?

When you forsake the world, you hate sin, read Galatians chapter five verse nineteen through verse twenty- two.

When we live in the works of the flesh, adultery, fornication, uncleanness, drunkenness, wrath, witchcraft, and hatred, we will not inherit the kingdom of God.

We need to ask ourselves, what do we need to forsake in our life, to gain all that God has for us. We must forsake the world to gain the kingdom.

To gain is to increase, advance and profit, to benefit on a greater level, having a surer reward.

Gaining the kingdom of God is to increase in a life of abundance, advancing to a higher level of maturity in him, becoming sons, obtaining all the benefits and promises of God, having a life of no lack, possessing more than enough, living in overflow.

Living in the kingdom of God, is rest, profiting from the word that is in your heart, having power to overcome the world, living above only, and never beneath, living in the power and favor of God, in the kingdom of righteousness, peace and joy.

Our abundant life is not just for ourselves, and when we increase in the fruits of the spirit, rivers of living waters flow into others, we represent the lord, benefitting from the increased word, which gives wisdom and knowledge, that directs our path to our destiny in the helping of others, our lives have an astounding effect on others.

We gain all of the kingdom, when we lose the world, yes, we do have to live in this world, but we certainly do not have to love what the sinful world has to offer.

"If any man loves the world, the love of the father is not in him." Read 1John 2:15

Another important aspect of kingdom living is our faith, we cannot please God without faith, we walk by faith, and not by sight, having faith is believing God, and knowing that he can do all things, nothing is to hard for him, we believe in our hearts, and confess with our mouth, having faith draws from the spirit realm, into the natural realm.

Forsaking all to gain all, is living the blessings of Abraham, I don't know about you, but I am headed in that direction.

On your journey, you will go through some things, but remember, you are only going through, to get to your destiny.

Why we go back to familiar things.

Familiar things can be people, toys, even games, these things are a comfort to us, that pacifier our ego, and feed our emotions with stuff that we are accustomed to, things we frequently are doing or are keeping in our lives, these things are habits, that have become a part of our behavior, that we do subconsciously on a regular basis, we have enjoyment in them, because of the comfort they give.

Familiar people or things can become very gratifying, these people or things are physically and mentally relaxing, forming us to becoming content, we find it easier to stay in the same environment than to make a conscience effort to step into the unknown.

When we pacifier ourselves, we bribe our self-esteem and our ability to do better. We try keeping the situation at our comfort zone, convincing ourselves we are happy and content, with not moving forward.

I have noticed so many times in my life, people (including myself) running back to things, circumstances, and places that seem so normal, those dead churches, back stabbing family members, even enemies they consider to be friends, some people go back to the games that only children play. So many of these things we find hard to depart from, we repetitively move in the same circles, we imprison our own ability to progress.

Never striving to move forward, we stay in the comfort of familiarity, never renewing our mind to redirect our thinking, we are living in the traditions and belief of only what we have perceived to be true.

Stop living in the traditions and beliefs of man and live by the word of God. Leave the familiar, habitual things alone, we must put our minds in subjection to the word of God long enough, for the word to perform in our life. Let us wait with patience, without wavering, understanding that these familiar things only hold us back from any progress that is needed, to take place in our lives.

At different circumstances in my life, I have returned back to people, places and things, because my ability to wait on the lord had faltered, we must learn to not waver, or feed our mind with comfort instead of truth, sometimes the lord has to remove all the things we are depending on, and trusting in, he will even stop you from attending certain places.

Step out of your comfort zone and stop struggling back and forth, start walking into the newness of your mind, began renewing your mind daily, on what the word of God says for your life, we must stop practicing what is familiar, and move ahead taking one step at a time, into the direction he is leading you in.

"For as many, as are led by the Spirit of God, they are the sons of God.

The Pattern of Christianity

Christians have a blueprint, the bible, it is our guide, our purpose to prepare us in executing the will of God in this earth.

Our strength of character is God's power working in us, it is his force and ability, molding and shaping, forming us into the ultimate pattern of becoming more like him each day, even our character constitutes, we are established in him.

Our pattern of Christianity is our belief, trust and confidence in his principles we live by, it is the certainty of having an assurance of his loyalty, knowing that God has the perfect blueprint for our life.

This pattern formulates our very existence, in our routine to become in the same similarities as him, his ways of doing things will keep us in route on the right path to our destiny.

We understand the work is already finished, completed before we were in our mother's womb, before the foundations of the world we were already in him, we were not just an afterthought, we were a living, predestined being in him.

Man is created in God's image, fashioned after his likeness, having every persona as his only begotten, for it is written "As he is, so are we in this world." His blood qualifies us.

We have surrendered all, accepting him as our beloved savior, healer, helper, protector and guide, he gives us joy and peace that surpasses our understanding, he is a safe haven in every storm, leading us to a higher way of thinking, to produce what he has placed in us, to execute his will in this earth. He is everything we need and more!

This is why we as Christians model and imitate ourselves after him, we become changed into the characteristics of our Lord and savior, when renewing our mind, we began changing, from the old into the newness of his thinking.

We leave our past behind, and press through the pain, hurt, and uncertainties of life, to finish our course, rising each time we fall, getting back up, entering into the set plan he has for our destiny, knowing it is finished.

Hear the word, be doers of the word, showing compassion at all times, not living by your emotions, but by the word of God, obeying and trusting in him and not man, these are the patterns we pursue in preparation of becoming the son's and daughters of God.

Ask yourself are you imitating Jesus?

Are you an example for others to see?

How bright is your light shining?

Do you pray daily, or only when trouble comes?

Have you forgiven everyone?

You look like a Christian, smell good like a Christian, dress like a Christian, except when I see you in the lottery line at the store, or when I overhear you cussing out the sales lady at the department store, and what about when I drove pass the club, I saw you coming out the door.

Are you an authentic Christian or a counterfeit?

It's time now, today to start living like the sons of God that we truly are, grow up out of the selfish, self-centered, self-seeking, self-interest, of your egotistic small mind, and look at the bigger picture of his plan for our life.

We are not waiting on God to make things happen, he is waiting on us to grow up and take our place in his kingdom, we must position ourselves in maturity, to develop a responsibility and commitment to the giving of ourselves, mind body and soul, having unfaltering faith.

Some seem to think they are blessed and prosperous, by the amount of money they have accumulated, prospered is so much more than just money as I stated in a previous chapter, it is good health, joy, peace, creativity, success, wealth, and the list goes on.

A Christian lifestyle is a pattern of Christianity we pursue, with a renewing of our mind over a course of our entire lives, it's a behavior we advance in continually developing to be more like Jesus, until it becomes our normal way of living.

We are going from glory to glory, to God!

CPSIA information can be obtained
at www.ICGtesting.com
Printed in the USA
BVHW031119150519
548352BV00007B/26/P